The Artistic Entrepreneur

A Student's Guide to Thriving in the Creative Industry

Merry Hail

The Artistic Entrepreneur A Student's Guide to Thriving in the Creative Industry
Copyright © 2023 by Merry Hail

The first edition was published in 2023

ISBN:

Published by:
Noya
1663 Liberty Drive
Hyderabad, IN 47403
www.noyapublishers.com

This book is self-published using on-demand printing and publishing, which allows it to be printed and distributed globally.

TABLE OF CONTENTS

Chapter 1: Exploring Your Creative Journey

Understanding the Creative Industry

In today's rapidly evolving world, the creative industry has emerged as 7a dynamic and vibrant field, offering endless opportunities for students looking to carve a successful career. This subchapter aims to provide students with a comprehensive understanding of the creative industry and its various facets, equipping them with the knowledge and insights needed to thrive in this exciting field.

The creative industry encompasses a wide range of disciplines, including visual arts, design, music, film, fashion, advertising, and more. It is a sector driven by creativity, innovation, and imagination, where individuals can transform their artistic talents into lucrative careers. Understanding the unique characteristics and dynamics of the creative industry is crucial for students aspiring to pursue a career in this field.

One key aspect of the creative industry is its ever-changing nature. Trends, technologies, and consumer preferences evolve rapidly, making it essential for students to stay updated with the latest developments. Embracing lifelong learning and being adaptable are vital qualities for success in this industry.

Moreover, the creative industry is characterized by a high level of competition. With numerous talented individuals vying for limited opportunities, students need to stand out from the crowd. Building a strong personal brand, showcasing a diverse portfolio, and networking with industry professionals are all essential strategies to gain a competitive edge.

Understanding the business side of the creative industry is equally important. Students need to comprehend the financial aspects, such as budgeting, pricing, and marketing, to ensure their creative endeavors are commercially viable. Learning about intellectual property rights, contracts, and negotiation skills is also crucial for protecting their work and securing fair opportunities.

Another significant aspect to consider is the multidisciplinary nature of the creative industry. Collaboration and cross-pollination between different creative fields often lead to innovative and groundbreaking work. Encouraging students to explore connections between their own discipline and others can open up new avenues and enhance their creative output.

In conclusion, the creative industry offers immense potential for students seeking a fulfilling and prosperous career. By understanding the unique characteristics, ever-changing nature, and business aspects of the creative industry, students can position themselves for success. Embracing lifelong learning, building a personal brand, and fostering collaboration are all essential strategies for thriving in this exciting field. With the right knowledge and mindset, students can embark on a journey as artistic entrepreneurs, transforming their passions into a thriving career in the creative industry.

Embracing Your Passion for Art

Art has the power to touch hearts, stimulate minds, and evoke emotions like no other medium. As students, you have the opportunity to explore and nurture your passion for art, and perhaps even turn it into a fulfilling career in the creative industry. This subchapter aims to guide you on the journey of embracing your passion for art and discovering the possibilities it holds for your future.

First and foremost, it is crucial to realize that pursuing a career in the arts requires dedication, persistence, and a willingness to step outside your comfort zone. The path may not always be easy, but if you truly love what you do, it will be worth every challenge and sacrifice along the way.

To embrace your passion for art, start by immersing yourself in various art forms. Experiment with different mediums such as painting, sculpture, photography, or digital art. Attend art exhibitions, visit galleries, and explore the works of renowned artists to broaden your artistic horizons. This exposure will help you develop a unique artistic perspective and inspire your own creations.

Furthermore, seek out opportunities to learn from experienced professionals in the field. Attend workshops, enroll in art classes, or even consider pursuing a degree in fine arts or a related discipline. Formal education will not only enhance your technical skills but also provide you with a deeper understanding of art history, theory, and criticism.

While honing your artistic abilities, it is equally important to develop an entrepreneurial mindset. The creative industry requires individuals who can navigate the business side of art, including marketing, networking, and managing finances. Recognize the value of your artwork and learn how to effectively promote it to potential clients or galleries.

In addition, embrace collaboration and networking opportunities. Connect with fellow artists, join art communities, and participate in collaborative projects. The creative industry thrives on collaboration, and by working with others, you can gain fresh perspectives, expand your network, and uncover new avenues for growth.

Remember, embracing your passion for art is not just about creating beautiful works; it is about finding your unique voice and making a meaningful impact through your art. By putting in the effort, staying true to yourself, and continually pushing your creative boundaries, you can forge a successful and fulfilling career in the art world.

So, let your imagination soar, your brush strokes dance, and your passion for art shine through every creation. Embrace the possibilities, nurture your talent, and become an artistic entrepreneur who thrives in the creative industry.

Identifying Your Creative Strengths and Interests

In today's rapidly evolving creative industry, it is crucial for students aspiring to pursue a career in this field to understand their own unique creative strengths and interests. Recognizing these qualities will not only help you find your niche but also enable you to thrive as an artistic entrepreneur. This subchapter aims to guide students in identifying their creative strengths and interests, laying the foundation for a successful and fulfilling creative career.

1. Self-Reflection: The first step in identifying your creative strengths and interests is self-reflection. Take the time to introspect and understand what aspects of the creative industry excite and inspire you the most. Consider the creative activities that bring you joy, whether it's painting, writing, photography, or design. Ask yourself what you excel at and what you are passionate about.

2. Skill Assessment: Evaluate your skills and abilities objectively. What are your natural talents? Are you skilled in visual arts, music, performing arts, or writing? Identify your strengths and weaknesses to determine which areas you can further develop and hone.

3. Experimentation: Explore various creative mediums and disciplines. Engage in different projects or internships to gain hands-on experience across different areas of the creative industry. This experimentation will help you discover new talents and interests, opening doors to unexpected possibilities.

4. Feedback and Critique: Seek feedback from mentors, teachers, and peers. Their insights can offer valuable perspectives on your creative strengths and areas that need improvement. Embrace constructive criticism as it will help refine your skills and push you to grow.

5. Research and Exploration: Immerse yourself in the world of creativity by researching successful artists and entrepreneurs. Discover the different career paths available within the creative industry. This exploration will help you identify potential areas where your creative strengths can be applied.

6. Passion and Longevity: Consider the creative pursuits that you can see yourself engaged in for the long term. Identify the activities that ignite a fire within you, as this passion will be the driving force behind your success as an artistic entrepreneur.

By identifying your creative strengths and interests, you will be able to carve a unique career path that aligns with your passions. This self-awareness will enable you to make informed decisions about the types of projects you pursue, the clients you work with, and the industries you enter. Remember, cultivating your creative strengths and interests is an ongoing process that requires continuous learning and adaptation. Embrace the journey, stay curious, and let your creativity soar in the ever-evolving world of the creative industry.

Chapter 2: Nurturing Your Artistic Talents

Developing Your Creative Skills

In the fast-paced and ever-evolving world of the creative industry, possessing strong creative skills is essential for any student looking to thrive in their career. Whether you aspire to be a visual artist, a designer, a writer, or any other creative professional, honing your creative skills is a continuous process that can significantly impact your success. This subchapter aims to guide students on how to develop and enhance their creative abilities, providing valuable insights and practical tips to help you unleash your creative potential.

1. Embrace your uniqueness: One of the most critical aspects of developing your creative skills is embracing your uniqueness. Recognize that your perspective and ideas are valuable and can set you apart from others. Embrace your individuality and let it shine through your work.

2. Seek inspiration: To nurture your creative abilities, expose yourself to a wide range of influences. Explore different art forms, read books, watch movies, listen to music, and engage with various cultures. This will broaden your horizons and provide you with a rich pool of inspiration to draw from.

3. Experiment and take risks: Creativity thrives on experimentation and taking risks. Don't be afraid to step out of your comfort zone and try new things. Push your boundaries,

challenge conventional thinking, and embrace failure as a learning opportunity.

4. Foster a creative mindset: Cultivate a mindset that embraces curiosity, open-mindedness, and adaptability. Embrace challenges and view them as opportunities for growth. Practice mindfulness and seek out environments that stimulate your creativity.

5. Practice regularly: Like any skill, creative abilities require practice to flourish. Dedicate time to your craft daily, even if it's just for a few minutes. Engage in creative exercises, sketch, write, or create something new every day. Consistency is key to progress.

6. Collaborate and seek feedback: Collaboration with peers and seeking feedback from mentors and professionals can be invaluable. Engaging in group projects and receiving constructive criticism can help you refine your creative skills and learn from others' expertise.

7. Stay updated and adapt: The creative industry is constantly evolving, so staying updated with the latest trends and technologies is crucial. Embrace new tools, software, and techniques to remain relevant and adaptable in your chosen field.

Remember, developing your creative skills is a lifelong journey. Don't get discouraged by setbacks or comparing yourself to others. Stay focused, persistent, and passionate about your craft. By nurturing your creative abilities, you'll be well-equipped to thrive in the dynamic and competitive world of the creative industry.

Honing Your Craft through Practice

In the vast and ever-evolving creative industry, one thing remains constant – the importance of practice. As a student pursuing a career in the creative field, whether it be art, music, writing, or any other artistic endeavor, honing your craft through practice is crucial to your success.

Practice is not merely about repetition; it is about dedicating time and effort to improve your skills and develop your unique artistic voice. It is through practice that you can refine your techniques, experiment with different styles, and grow as an artist.

First and foremost, it is essential to set aside regular time for practice. Treat it as a sacred ritual, a time to focus solely on your craft. Create a schedule that works for you, whether it's dedicating a few hours each day or setting aside specific days of the week for practice. Consistency is key – make it a habit, and you'll see the results.

When practicing, consider challenging yourself. Push beyond your comfort zone and experiment with new ideas and techniques. Embrace failure as a learning opportunity and don't be afraid to make mistakes. It is through these experiences that you will discover new avenues for creativity and grow as an artist.

Additionally, seek feedback and guidance from mentors, teachers, or peers. Constructive criticism is invaluable in helping you identify areas for improvement and gain a fresh perspective on your work. Embrace feedback with an open mind, and remember that it is not a reflection of your worth as an artist but rather an opportunity for growth.

Incorporating deliberate practice techniques can also enhance your progress. Focus on specific aspects of your craft and break them down into manageable tasks. For example, if you are a writer, practice creating compelling characters or writing engaging dialogue. By isolating and working on individual skills, you can strengthen your overall abilities.

Lastly, don't forget the power of patience and perseverance. Progress may be slow, and there will be moments of frustration, but remember that every great artist started as a student. Embrace the journey and enjoy the process of honing your craft.

In conclusion, honing your craft through practice is essential for any student aspiring to thrive in the creative industry. Dedicate time, challenge yourself, seek feedback, and embrace deliberate practice techniques. Remember, the road to success is paved with practice, patience, and a passion for your art. Stay committed, and you will undoubtedly see your skills and career flourish.

Seeking Feedback and Constructive Criticism

In the fast-paced and ever-evolving world of the creative industry, the ability to seek feedback and learn from constructive criticism is crucial for any aspiring student looking to build a successful career. Whether you are an artist, musician, writer, or designer, understanding how to effectively navigate feedback can propel your growth and development as an artistic entrepreneur.

Feedback is not always easy to receive, especially when it comes to something as personal and subjective as art. However, embracing feedback can be a powerful tool for improvement and innovation. It provides an external perspective, highlighting areas where you can refine your skills and refine your work to resonate better with your intended audience.

First and foremost, it is important to approach feedback with an open mind and a growth mindset. Remember that feedback is not a personal attack but an opportunity for growth. Be receptive to different viewpoints and opinions, even if they challenge your initial vision. Embrace the idea that constructive criticism can help you refine your artistic voice and push your creative boundaries.

When seeking feedback, it is crucial to choose the right people to provide it. Reach out to mentors, professors, industry professionals, or fellow students who have a deep understanding of your niche and can offer valuable insights. Surrounding yourself with a supportive network of individuals who genuinely want to see you succeed is essential.

Additionally, be specific about the feedback you are seeking. Clearly communicate what aspects of your work you would like feedback on, whether it's composition, technique, storytelling, or audience appeal. This will help guide the conversation and ensure that you receive targeted feedback that can truly enhance your creative output.

Once you receive feedback, take the time to reflect on it. Avoid becoming defensive or dismissive of suggestions that may challenge your original ideas. Instead, carefully analyze the feedback and consider how it aligns with your artistic goals. Remember, you have the power to decide which feedback to incorporate and which to discard. Trust your instincts and intuition, while also being open to experimenting and taking calculated risks.

Lastly, remember that seeking feedback is an ongoing process. As you grow and evolve as an artistic entrepreneur, continue to seek feedback and surround yourself with individuals who will push you to reach new heights. Embrace the journey of continuous improvement, and you will find yourself thriving in the creative industry.

In conclusion, seeking feedback and constructive criticism is an invaluable skill for any student aspiring to succeed in a creative career. Embrace feedback with an open mind, choose the right people to provide it, be specific in what you seek, reflect on the feedback, and continuously seek growth. By developing this skill, you will elevate your artistic abilities, refine your work, and ultimately thrive in the dynamic world of the creative industry.

Chapter 3: Building a Personal Brand as an Artist

Defining Your Unique Artistic Identity

In the creative industry, where competition is fierce and opportunities are limited, it is vital for students aspiring to build a successful career as artistic entrepreneurs to define their unique artistic identity. Your artistic identity is what sets you apart from others, showcases your individuality, and becomes your signature style. It is the essence of who you are as an artist and will play a significant role in shaping your career trajectory.

So, how can you define your unique artistic identity?

1. Reflection and Self-Discovery: Take the time to reflect on your personal experiences, values, and passions. What are the themes that resonate with you? What are the emotions you want to evoke through your art? Understanding yourself on a deeper level will help you develop a unique artistic voice.

2. Experimentation: Don't be afraid to step out of your comfort zone and explore different mediums, techniques, and styles. Experimentation allows you to discover new ways to express yourself and adds depth to your artistic identity.

3. Embrace Your Influences: Every artist is influenced by others. Study the works of your favorite artists, both historical and contemporary, and learn from their techniques and approaches. However, it is essential to find a balance between being inspired by others and finding your own authentic voice.

4. Consistency and Practice: Consistency is key in developing your artistic identity. Set aside dedicated time for creating art and practice regularly. By doing so, you will refine your skills, gain confidence, and gradually establish a recognizable style that reflects your artistic identity.

5. Feedback and Reflection: Seek feedback from mentors, peers, and industry professionals. Constructive criticism can help you identify strengths and areas for improvement, ultimately shaping your artistic identity. Reflect on the feedback you receive and use it to refine your work.

6. Authenticity: Be true to yourself and let your art reflect your unique perspective. Trying to imitate others or catering solely to market trends may lead to short-term success but can hinder the development of your authentic artistic identity in the long run.

Remember, defining your unique artistic identity is an ongoing process. It evolves as you grow and gain more experience. Embrace the journey, stay open to new ideas, and always strive to push the boundaries of your creativity. Your unique artistic identity will be the cornerstone of your career as an artistic entrepreneur, enabling you to stand out in a crowded industry and attract opportunities that align with your vision.

Showcasing Your Artwork and Portfolio

In today's competitive creative industry, having a strong portfolio is crucial for students looking to establish a successful career as an artistic entrepreneur. Your portfolio is not only a compilation of your best work but also a representation of your unique artistic voice and capabilities. It serves as a visual resume, allowing potential clients and employers to assess your skills, creativity, and suitability for their specific needs. This subchapter will guide you on how to effectively showcase your artwork and portfolio to make a lasting impression on your target audience.

First and foremost, it is essential to curate your portfolio thoughtfully. Select your best and most representative pieces, showcasing your range and versatility within your chosen niche. Include a variety of mediums, styles, and themes that highlight your strengths as an artist. Remember, quality over quantity is key. A concise and well-curated portfolio will leave a stronger impact than a cluttered one.

Consider the format of your portfolio. In today's digital age, having an online portfolio is a must. Create a visually appealing and user-friendly website to showcase your work. Ensure that your website is easy to navigate and that your artwork is displayed in high resolution. Don't forget to include a brief artist statement and contact information for potential clients or employers to reach out.

In addition to your online presence, consider other platforms to showcase your artwork. Participate in local art exhibitions, galleries, and art fairs to gain exposure and network with industry professionals. Additionally, social media platforms such as Instagram and Pinterest can be powerful tools to promote your work. Regularly share your artwork, engage with your audience, and collaborate with other artists to expand your reach.

Lastly, continually update and refine your portfolio. As you grow and experiment with your artistic style, it is important to keep your portfolio up-to-date. Remove any outdated or weaker pieces and replace them with your latest and most compelling work. Continuously seek feedback from your peers, mentors, and industry professionals to ensure that your portfolio is always evolving and reflecting your current artistic journey.

Remember, your portfolio is your gateway to a successful career as an artistic entrepreneur. It is a reflection of your creativity, skills, and dedication to your craft. Invest time and effort into curating a strong and compelling portfolio that showcases your unique artistic voice. With a well-presented portfolio, you will stand out in the competitive creative industry and open doors to exciting opportunities for your career.

Utilizing Social Media and Online Platforms for Self-Promotion

In today's digital age, social media and online platforms have become powerful tools for self-promotion and building a successful career in the creative industry. As students aspiring to thrive in this competitive field, understanding how to effectively leverage these platforms is essential. This subchapter will explore the various ways in which you can utilize social media and online platforms to promote your artistry and establish a strong personal brand.

First and foremost, it's crucial to have a clear understanding of your target audience. Identify who your work resonates with and tailor your online presence accordingly. Whether you're a photographer, musician, writer, or visual artist, having a specific niche will help you connect with the right audience who appreciates and supports your work.

One of the most popular and versatile platforms for self-promotion is social media. Platforms like Instagram, Facebook, Twitter, and LinkedIn allow you to showcase your work, engage with your audience, and network with industry professionals. Create a consistent and visually appealing feed that reflects your unique style and aesthetic. Regularly post high-quality content, including behind-the-scenes glimpses, works in progress, and finished pieces. Engage with your followers by responding to comments, participating in discussions, and supporting other artists within your community.

Additionally, consider joining online communities and forums that cater to your specific niche. Platforms like Behance, Dribbble, and SoundCloud provide opportunities to showcase your portfolio, receive feedback, and connect with fellow artists and industry experts. Participating in these communities not only helps you gain exposure but also provides valuable networking opportunities that can lead to collaboration and career advancement.

Another effective strategy for self-promotion is creating and maintaining a personal website or blog. This serves as a central hub for your work, allowing you to establish your brand and showcase your portfolio in a professional manner. Update your website regularly with new projects, blog posts, and testimonials to provide visitors with a comprehensive view of your skills and expertise.

Lastly, don't underestimate the power of video content. Platforms like YouTube, TikTok, and Vimeo offer unique opportunities to showcase your creative process, share tutorials, and engage with a wider audience. Consider creating engaging and informative videos that not only highlight your work but also provide value to your viewers.

In conclusion, social media and online platforms offer endless possibilities for self-promotion and career growth. By understanding your target audience, creating a strong personal brand, and utilizing these platforms effectively, you can take your artistic career to new heights. Embrace the digital landscape, stay consistent, and never underestimate the power of genuine engagement. The creative industry is waiting for your unique voice to be heard.

Chapter 4: Entrepreneurial Mindset for Success

Embracing the Role of an Artistic Entrepreneur

In today's ever-evolving creative industry, it is crucial for students pursuing a career in the arts to embrace the role of an artistic entrepreneur. Gone are the days when artists solely focused on their craft; now, they must also possess a business mindset and entrepreneurial spirit to thrive in this competitive landscape.

As a student, you may wonder what it means to be an artistic entrepreneur. Simply put, it refers to taking charge of your artistic career and leveraging your skills and creativity to create a sustainable livelihood. It involves thinking outside the box, seizing opportunities, and actively seeking ways to monetize your art.

One of the key aspects of being an artistic entrepreneur is understanding the value of your work. As an artist, you bring a unique perspective and skill set to the table, and it is essential to recognize the worth of your creations. This mindset shift can help you confidently negotiate fair compensation for your work and resist the temptation to undervalue your talent.

Another vital aspect of embracing the role of an artistic entrepreneur is developing a strong business acumen. While creativity is the backbone of your artistic pursuits, understanding the business side of the industry is equally important. This includes learning about marketing, finance, networking, and project management. By acquiring these skills, you can effectively promote and sell your work, manage your finances, and build a robust professional network.

Furthermore, as an artistic entrepreneur, it is crucial to embrace innovation and adaptability. The creative industry is constantly evolving, and it is essential to stay ahead of the curve. Embracing new technologies, exploring different mediums, and seeking out unconventional collaborations can help you stand out from the crowd and foster a competitive edge.

Lastly, as a student, it is essential to cultivate a growth mindset and be open to learning from both successes and failures. Being an artistic entrepreneur is a journey filled with ups and downs, and it is through these experiences that you gain valuable insights and refine your craft. Embrace feedback, continuously seek self-improvement, and be willing to take calculated risks.

In conclusion, embracing the role of an artistic entrepreneur is vital for students pursuing a career in the creative industry. By recognizing the value of your work, developing a business mindset, embracing innovation, and cultivating a growth mindset, you can position yourself for success in this dynamic field. Remember, being an artistic entrepreneur is not just about creating art; it is about harnessing your creativity to thrive as a professional in the creative industry.

Cultivating a Growth Mindset

In today's fast-paced and ever-evolving world, the ability to adapt and embrace change is crucial for success in any career, especially in the creative industry. This subchapter aims to explore the concept of cultivating a growth mindset, offering valuable insights and strategies to help students thrive in their creative careers.

A growth mindset is the belief that one's abilities and intelligence can be developed through dedication, hard work, and continuous learning. It is a mindset that encourages individuals to see challenges as opportunities for growth, rather than obstacles to be avoided. As students embark on their journey into the creative industry, adopting a growth mindset can be the key to unlocking their full potential and realizing their aspirations.

One significant aspect of cultivating a growth mindset is the willingness to embrace failure and learn from it. In the creative industry, setbacks and failures are inevitable, but they should be viewed as valuable learning experiences rather than reasons to give up. Students must understand that failure is not a reflection of their abilities, but rather a stepping stone towards improvement. By reframing failures as opportunities for growth, students can develop resilience and perseverance, essential qualities in any successful career.

Additionally, fostering a growth mindset involves seeking out new challenges and stepping outside of one's comfort zone. The creative industry is constantly evolving, and staying stagnant can hinder progress. Students must be open to exploring new techniques, technologies, and ideas, pushing themselves to acquire new skills and expand their horizons. By embracing challenges and seeking continuous improvement, students can stay ahead of the curve and thrive in their creative careers.

Furthermore, developing a growth mindset requires the cultivation of a passion for lifelong learning. In the creative industry, trends and technologies are constantly changing, and it is essential to stay updated and adaptable. Students should actively seek out opportunities for learning, whether through workshops, online courses, or networking events. By embracing a love for learning and seeking new knowledge, students can stay relevant and continually evolve in their chosen career path.

In conclusion, cultivating a growth mindset is essential for students in the creative industry. By embracing failure as a learning opportunity, seeking out challenges, and fostering a passion for lifelong learning, students can position themselves for success in their creative careers. The ability to adapt, learn, and grow is crucial in a rapidly changing world, and a growth mindset is the key to thriving in the dynamic and ever-evolving creative industry.

Overcoming Self-Doubt and Fear of Failure

Introduction:

In the journey towards a successful career in the creative industry, one common obstacle that often stands in the way of students is self-doubt and fear of failure. These negative emotions can paralyze us, preventing us from taking risks, pursuing our dreams, and reaching our full potential. However, with the right mindset and strategies, it is possible to overcome these challenges and thrive as an artistic entrepreneur.

1. Understanding Self-Doubt:
Self-doubt is a natural part of the human experience, particularly when venturing into a new career path. It is important to recognize that everyone, even the most accomplished individuals, has moments of self-doubt. By understanding that these feelings are universal, students can begin to reframe their perspective and realize that they are not alone in their struggles.

2. Identifying the Root Causes:
To effectively overcome self-doubt and fear of failure, students must identify the underlying causes of these emotions. Often, it is a result of comparing oneself to others, setting unrealistic expectations, or a lack of confidence in one's abilities. By pinpointing the root causes, students can begin to address and challenge these negative beliefs.

3. Cultivating Self-Compassion:
Self-compassion is a powerful tool in overcoming self-doubt. Students should learn to treat themselves with kindness and

understanding, just as they would a friend facing similar challenges. By practicing self-compassion, students can develop resilience and bounce back from setbacks with greater ease.

4. Embracing Failure as a Learning Opportunity: Failure is an inevitable part of any career journey, particularly in the creative industry. Instead of fearing failure, students should embrace it as an opportunity for growth and learning. By reframing failure as a stepping stone to success, students can develop a resilient mindset that allows them to persevere in the face of adversity.

5. Building a Supportive Network: Surrounding oneself with a supportive network of mentors, peers, and industry professionals is crucial in overcoming self-doubt and fear of failure. By seeking guidance and feedback from trusted individuals, students can gain valuable insights, encouragement, and motivation to push through their challenges.

Conclusion:

Overcoming self-doubt and fear of failure is an essential skill for any aspiring artistic entrepreneur. By understanding the nature of self-doubt, identifying its root causes, cultivating self-compassion, embracing failure, and building a supportive network, students can empower themselves to confidently pursue their creative careers. Remember, success often comes from taking risks and pushing past our limitations. With determination and the right mindset, you can overcome self-doubt and fear of failure and thrive in the creative industry.

Chapter 5: Financial Management for Creative Professionals

Understanding the Business Side of the Creative Industry

In today's rapidly evolving world, creativity and innovation have become essential skills for success. The creative industry, which encompasses fields such as art, design, music, film, and writing, offers countless opportunities for talented individuals to pursue fulfilling careers. However, being successful in the creative industry goes beyond just talent and passion; it requires a solid understanding of the business side of things.

This subchapter aims to shed light on the business aspects of the creative industry and provide students with valuable insights to help them thrive in their future careers. While many students are drawn to the creative industry for its artistic freedom and personal expression, it is crucial to remember that it is also an industry driven by market demands and financial considerations.

One key aspect to understand is the importance of creating a personal brand. Just like any other business, individuals in the creative industry need to differentiate themselves from the competition. Building a strong personal brand that showcases your unique talents, style, and values is essential for attracting clients, employers, or fans. This subchapter will explore various strategies for creating a compelling personal brand and developing an online presence that reflects your creative identity.

Another crucial topic to be covered is the financial side of the creative industry. Students need to understand how to monetize their talents and navigate the challenges of pricing their work, negotiating contracts, and managing finances. This subchapter will provide practical tips and advice on how to set fair prices, protect intellectual property rights, and establish healthy financial habits to ensure long-term success in the creative industry.

Moreover, students will gain insights into networking and collaboration, which are fundamental for career growth in the creative industry. Building a strong professional network, attending industry events, and collaborating with other creative professionals can open doors to new opportunities and help students stay updated with industry trends. This subchapter will guide students on how to cultivate meaningful connections and foster collaborations that can enhance their creative journey.

Understanding the business side of the creative industry is essential for students who want to turn their passion into a sustainable career. By equipping themselves with knowledge about personal branding, finance management, and networking, students can navigate the competitive landscape of the creative industry and thrive in their chosen niche. With the right balance of artistic talent and business acumen, students can become artistic entrepreneurs who not only create remarkable work but also build successful and fulfilling careers in the creative industry.

Budgeting and Financial Planning as an Artist

In the dynamic and ever-evolving world of creative industries, understanding the importance of budgeting and financial planning is crucial for aspiring artists. While talent and creativity are undoubtedly essential, managing your finances effectively can greatly contribute to a successful and sustainable career in the arts. This subchapter aims to equip students pursuing a career in the creative industry with the necessary knowledge and skills to navigate the financial aspects of their artistic journey.

Budgeting serves as the foundation for financial planning and involves carefully allocating your income and expenses. As an artist, it is essential to determine your sources of income, such as freelance work, grants, sales, or commissions. Creating a realistic budget allows you to keep track of your earnings and expenses, ensuring that your artistic pursuits remain financially viable.

One crucial aspect of financial planning as an artist is understanding the concept of irregular income. Unlike traditional salaried jobs, artists often experience fluctuating income streams. Learning to manage irregular income requires discipline and foresight. Setting aside a portion of your earnings during prosperous times can help sustain you during lean periods and provide a financial safety net.

Moreover, it is vital to prioritize expenses and make conscious financial decisions. Differentiate between essential expenses, such as art supplies, studio rent, or professional development, and discretionary spending. By distinguishing between needs and wants, you can allocate your funds accordingly, ensuring that your artistic practice remains financially sustainable.

Additionally, financial planning involves setting long-term goals and establishing strategies to achieve them. These goals may include saving for a solo exhibition, investing in new equipment, or building a retirement fund. By setting clear objectives and implementing a savings plan, you can work towards achieving your artistic aspirations while securing your financial future.

Furthermore, understanding the tax implications for artists is paramount. Familiarize yourself with tax laws and regulations specific to the creative industry, as they often differ from traditional employment. Seek guidance from experts in this field to ensure you comply with tax requirements and take advantage of any applicable deductions or credits.

In conclusion, budgeting and financial planning are indispensable skills for artists embarking on a career in the creative industry. By mastering these skills, students can navigate the financial challenges that come with irregular income, prioritize expenses, set goals, and secure their financial well-being. Remember, while creativity is the heart of your artistic journey, effective financial management will provide the stability required to thrive in the competitive world of the arts.

Exploring Different Revenue Streams for Artists

In today's rapidly changing creative industry, artists need to adopt a multifaceted approach to generate income and sustain a successful career. Gone are the days when artists relied solely on selling their artwork or receiving commissions. In this subchapter, we will explore various revenue streams that artists can tap into to thrive in the creative industry.

1. Selling Artwork: This traditional revenue stream involves selling original pieces, prints, or limited editions directly to collectors, galleries, or through online platforms. Artists can also participate in art fairs and exhibitions to reach a wider audience.

2. Commissions: Artists can secure commissioned projects from individuals, organizations, or businesses. This could involve creating custom artworks, murals, illustrations, or designs for various purposes, such as branding, book covers, or album art.

3. Licensing and Merchandising: Artists can explore licensing their artwork for use on various products like apparel, home decor, stationery, or even digital platforms. Creating merchandise such as prints, posters, calendars, or even designing products like clothing or accessories can also generate additional revenue.

4. Teaching and Workshops: Many artists find success in sharing their skills and knowledge by offering art classes, workshops, or online tutorials. This not only provides a steady income but also helps build a strong network and enhances their reputation as an expert in their field.

5. Collaborations and Partnerships: Artists can collaborate with other creative professionals, brands, or organizations to create unique projects or products. This could involve joint exhibitions, creating limited edition collections, or collaborating with fashion designers, musicians, or filmmakers.

6. Grants and Residencies: Artists can explore opportunities provided by government organizations, foundations, or art institutions that offer grants, fellowships, or artist residencies. These programs not only provide financial support but also offer valuable exposure and networking opportunities.

7. Digital Platforms: With the rise of online platforms, artists can showcase and sell their work through websites, online galleries, social media, or even crowdfunding platforms. This allows artists to reach a global audience and connect directly with potential buyers.

8. Art Therapy and Community Projects: Artists can contribute to society by working on art therapy programs, community-based projects, or public art installations. These initiatives not only provide a sense of fulfillment but can also attract funding or sponsorships from organizations that support such endeavors.

In conclusion, artists need to explore and embrace multiple revenue streams to thrive in the creative industry. By diversifying their income sources, artists can not only increase their financial stability but also expand their network, gain exposure, and build a sustainable and fulfilling career in the arts.

Chapter 6: Networking and Collaboration in the Creative Industry

Building a Supportive Network of Peers and Mentors

In the competitive and ever-evolving creative industry, having a strong support system is crucial for success. As students embarking on a career in the creative field, it is essential to build a network of peers and mentors who can guide, inspire, and support you throughout your journey. This subchapter delves into the importance of cultivating such a network and provides practical tips on how to do so effectively.

A supportive network of peers and mentors can provide numerous benefits to aspiring artists and entrepreneurs. Firstly, they offer a safe space for sharing ideas, experiences, and challenges. Surrounding yourself with like-minded individuals who understand the intricacies of the creative industry can be immensely comforting and motivating. Through group discussions, brainstorming sessions, and collaborations, you can gain fresh perspectives and find innovative solutions to the obstacles you may face.

Mentors, on the other hand, can provide invaluable guidance and wisdom derived from their own experiences in the industry. Their knowledge can help you navigate through the complex landscape of the creative world, offering insights that textbooks and classrooms may not provide. A mentor can help you identify your strengths, hone your skills, and provide advice on various aspects of your career, such as portfolio development, networking, and self-promotion.

To start building your network, begin by actively participating in your academic institution's creative clubs, organizations, or societies. These groups often provide a platform for collaboration and can connect you with fellow students who share your passion. Attend workshops, seminars, and industry events to expand your network beyond the confines of your school. Engaging with professionals in your desired field can open doors to potential mentors who can guide you towards your goals.

Utilize online platforms and social media to connect with peers and mentors worldwide. Online communities, forums, and social networks dedicated to the creative industry can be excellent resources for finding like-minded individuals and mentors who are willing to offer guidance remotely.

Remember, building a supportive network is a two-way street. Be generous with your own knowledge and experiences, as cultivating genuine relationships requires mutual support and encouragement. Be open to sharing ideas, offering feedback, and collaborating with your peers. Respect and value the expertise of your mentors, and always express gratitude for their guidance.

In conclusion, building a supportive network of peers and mentors is an essential aspect of thriving in the creative industry. By surrounding yourself with like-minded individuals and seeking guidance from experienced mentors, you can gain valuable insights, stay motivated, and create opportunities for professional growth. Take the initiative to connect with others, both in person and through online platforms, and remember to contribute your own knowledge and support to foster meaningful relationships.

Collaborating with Other Artists and Professionals

In the ever-evolving world of the creative industry, collaboration is not just a buzzword; it is a vital component of success. As a student aspiring to thrive in your creative career, understanding the power and potential of collaborating with other artists and professionals is essential.

Collaboration can take various forms, from working with fellow artists on a joint project to partnering with professionals from different fields to enhance your creative output. By embracing collaboration, you open yourself up to a world of opportunities and unlock new levels of creativity.

One of the most significant advantages of collaborating with other artists is the ability to tap into a diverse range of perspectives and skill sets. Each artist brings their unique background, experiences, and artistic style to the table, enriching the creative process. This diversity can lead to groundbreaking ideas and innovative solutions that you may not have discovered on your own. By collaborating, you can push the boundaries of your creativity and create work that resonates with a broader audience.

Collaboration also provides a platform for learning and growth. Working with other artists and professionals exposes you to different techniques, mediums, and ways of thinking. It allows you to expand your repertoire, acquire new skills, and gain a deeper understanding of your craft. Additionally, collaborating with professionals from other fields, such as marketing, business, or technology, can provide valuable insights into the industry and help you navigate the complex world of creative entrepreneurship.

Building a collaborative network is another crucial aspect of your artistic journey. Surrounding yourself with like-minded individuals who share your passion and ambition can be a source of inspiration, support, and motivation. Collaborating with peers and mentors can open doors to new opportunities, such as exhibitions, gigs, or commissions, that may not have been available to you otherwise.

However, successful collaboration requires effective communication, mutual respect, and a shared vision. It is essential to establish clear goals, roles, and expectations from the outset to ensure a smooth and productive collaboration. Additionally, open-mindedness, flexibility, and a willingness to compromise are key to navigating creative differences and finding common ground.

In conclusion, collaborating with other artists and professionals is a powerful tool for students looking to thrive in their creative careers. By embracing collaboration, you can tap into a diverse range of perspectives, learn and grow from others, expand your network, and create innovative work that stands out in the competitive creative industry. So, reach out, connect, and collaborate – the possibilities are endless!

Leveraging Networking Opportunities for Career Advancement

In today's competitive job market, networking has become an essential skill for advancing one's career. Whether you are a student or a seasoned professional, building a strong network can open doors to new opportunities and help you thrive in the creative industry. This subchapter explores the art of networking and provides valuable insights on how to leverage networking opportunities for career advancement.

Networking is not just about exchanging business cards or attending networking events; it is about building genuine relationships and connections. As a student, you have a unique advantage when it comes to networking. Your peers, professors, and alumni can become valuable resources in your career journey. Take advantage of your school's networking events, career fairs, and alumni associations to connect with professionals in your field of interest.

To make the most of networking opportunities, it is crucial to approach them with a strategic mindset. Before attending an event or reaching out to someone, do your research. Identify individuals or organizations that align with your career goals and interests. This will help you engage in more meaningful conversations and make a lasting impression.

Networking is not just about what you can gain; it is also about what you can offer. Be proactive in sharing your knowledge, skills, and experiences with others. By providing value to your network, you build trust and credibility, positioning yourself as a valuable asset to potential employers or collaborators.

Online platforms have revolutionized networking, offering endless opportunities to connect with professionals worldwide. Utilize platforms like LinkedIn, Behance, or industry-specific forums to expand your network beyond your immediate surroundings. Engage in online communities, join relevant groups, and participate in discussions to showcase your expertise and connect with like-minded individuals.

Remember, networking is an ongoing process. It requires consistent effort and nurturing relationships over time. Stay in touch with your contacts, follow up after meetings or events, and express gratitude for any assistance or advice received. Building a strong network takes time, but the rewards are immeasurable.

In conclusion, networking is a powerful tool for career advancement in the creative industry. As a student, take advantage of the networking opportunities available to you, both on and offline. Approach networking strategically, offering value and building genuine relationships. Nurture your network over time, and don't be afraid to reach out for guidance or support. By leveraging networking opportunities, you can pave the way for a successful and fulfilling career in the creative industry.

Chapter 7: Marketing and Selling Your Artwork

Developing a Marketing Strategy for Artists

In the ever-evolving world of the creative industry, artists must not only possess exceptional talent and creativity but also have a solid understanding of marketing strategies. Recognizing the importance of marketing for artists, this subchapter aims to equip students aspiring for a career in the creative industry with the necessary skills and knowledge to develop an effective marketing strategy.

First and foremost, it is crucial for artists to identify their target audience. Understanding who your work appeals to allows you to tailor your marketing efforts towards the right demographic. Researching and analyzing your target audience's preferences, interests, and buying behaviors can provide valuable insights into how to effectively reach and engage with them.

Once you have identified your target audience, it is essential to build a strong online presence. Utilize various digital platforms such as websites, social media, and online portfolios to showcase your work. Create a visually appealing and user-friendly website that highlights your portfolio, bio, and contact information. Social media platforms can also serve as powerful tools to connect with your audience, share behind-the-scenes glimpses of your creative process, and promote upcoming projects or events.

Collaboration is another key aspect of developing a marketing strategy for artists. Partnering with other artists, influencers, or organiżations can help expand your reach and expose your work to a wider audience. Consider collaborating on joint projects, participating in group exhibitions, or organizing workshops and events together. By combining your networks and resources, you can leverage each other's strengths and create mutually beneficial opportunities.

In addition to online marketing efforts, don't underestimate the power of traditional marketing methods. Attend industry events, art fairs, and exhibitions to network with professionals in the field. Explore opportunities for print advertising in relevant magazines or newspapers. Building relationships with art galleries, curators, and collectors can also open doors to new opportunities and increase your visibility within the art community.

Lastly, regularly evaluate and adapt your marketing strategy to align with industry trends and changing consumer behaviors. Stay updated on emerging technologies, social media algorithms, and marketing tools to ensure your efforts remain relevant and effective. By continuously refining your marketing strategy, you can position yourself as a professional artist who is not only creatively talented but also business-savvy.

In conclusion, developing a marketing strategy is imperative for artists aiming to forge a successful career in the creative industry. By understanding your target audience, building an online presence, collaborating with others, utilizing traditional marketing methods, and adapting to industry trends, you can effectively promote your work and thrive as an artistic entrepreneur.

Creating an Effective Artist Statement and Bio

In the competitive world of the creative industry, a well-crafted artist statement and bio can be powerful tools for students looking to establish a successful career. These two elements are essential for showcasing your artistic identity, communicating your vision, and capturing the attention of potential clients and galleries.

An artist statement is a concise and thoughtful description of your artistic practice. It serves as a window into your creative process, inspirations, and motivations. When crafting your artist statement, it's important to strike a balance between being authentic and engaging your audience. Start by reflecting on your work and identifying the themes, ideas, or concepts that drive your artistic expression. Consider how your art relates to the world, society, or personal experiences. Use descriptive language and vivid imagery to create a narrative that captivates the reader. Keep the statement concise and avoid jargon or technical terms that may alienate your audience. Remember, the goal is to provide a glimpse into your artistic world, not to overwhelm or confuse.

Equally important is your artist bio, which gives a brief overview of your background, achievements, and artistic journey. This section should highlight your education, exhibitions, awards, and any relevant experiences. When writing your artist bio, focus on showcasing your unique qualities and accomplishments. Include a personal touch by sharing the story of how you discovered your passion for art and your artistic influences. Remember to keep the bio concise and relevant. Potential clients and galleries want to know who you are as an artist, so make sure to emphasize your artistic voice and style.

Both the artist statement and bio should be regularly updated as your career progresses. As a student, it's crucial to continually refine and polish these documents to reflect your growth and evolving artistic identity. Seek feedback from mentors, professors, and peers to ensure that your statements effectively capture your artistic essence.

In conclusion, an effective artist statement and bio are indispensable tools for students pursuing a career in the creative industry. Crafted with care and authenticity, these elements will help you stand out, communicate your vision, and connect with potential clients and galleries. By investing time and effort into creating compelling statements, you will be well on your way to thriving as an artistic entrepreneur.

Approaching Galleries, Exhibitions, and Art Fairs

As a student pursuing a career in the creative industry, one of the most crucial aspects of your journey will involve engaging with galleries, exhibitions, and art fairs. These platforms not only provide opportunities to showcase your talent and gain recognition but also serve as significant networking hubs for artists, collectors, and art enthusiasts. In this subchapter, we will delve into some essential strategies and tips to help you effectively approach galleries, exhibitions, and art fairs.

1. Research and Identify Suitable Opportunities: Before approaching any gallery, exhibition, or art fair, conduct thorough research to identify the ones that align with your artistic style, medium, and career goals. Look for galleries that represent artists working in a similar genre or niche. Consider the reputation, clientele, and overall aesthetic of the gallery or event. This will ensure that your work is well-suited to the platform you are targeting.

2. Create a Professional Portfolio: A well-curated portfolio is your ticket to catching the attention of gallery owners, curators, and potential buyers. Make sure your portfolio showcases your best and most recent work, highlighting your unique style. Include a concise artist statement that effectively communicates your artistic vision and inspiration. Ensure that your portfolio is easily accessible in both physical and digital formats.

3. Networking and Relationship Building: Attend art exhibitions, openings, and art fairs to network with industry professionals.

Introduce yourself to gallery owners, curators, and fellow artists. Engage in meaningful conversations and express genuine interest in their work. Building relationships with people in the industry can open doors to future opportunities and collaborations.

4. Submitting Artwork Proposals: Many galleries and exhibitions accept artwork proposals from artists. When submitting a proposal, make sure to follow the guidelines provided by the gallery or event organizers. Tailor your proposal to fit the specific theme or focus of the exhibition. Include high-quality images of your artwork along with a detailed description of each piece.

5. Professionalism and Persistence: Approach galleries and exhibitions with a professional attitude. Be prepared to handle rejections and setbacks, as they are a common part of the artistic journey. Take feedback constructively and use it to improve your work. Stay persistent and keep exploring new opportunities.

Remember, the art world can be highly competitive, and success may not come overnight. However, with dedication, perseverance, and a strategic approach to approaching galleries, exhibitions, and art fairs, you can increase your chances of thriving in the creative industry.

Chapter 8: Balancing Creativity and Business

Managing Time and Priorities as a Creative Entrepreneur

As a creative entrepreneur, one of the key skills you need to master is time management. The ability to effectively manage your time and prioritize tasks is crucial for success in the fast-paced and demanding creative industry. In this subchapter, we will explore various strategies and techniques to help you make the most of your time and stay on top of your priorities.

First and foremost, it is essential to understand the value of time. Time is a limited resource, and as a creative entrepreneur, your time is your most valuable asset. Recognize that every minute you spend on non-essential tasks is a minute taken away from pursuing your creative goals and building your career.

To effectively manage your time, start by setting clear goals and objectives. Define what you want to achieve in both the short and long term. Break these goals down into smaller, actionable tasks that can be easily scheduled and accomplished. By having a clear roadmap, you will be able to allocate your time efficiently and stay focused on what truly matters.

Another important aspect of time management is setting priorities. As a creative entrepreneur, you will face numerous tasks and projects competing for your attention. It becomes crucial to identify and prioritize those tasks that align with your goals and have the highest impact on your career. Learn to differentiate between urgent and important tasks and tackle them accordingly.

Embracing productivity tools and techniques can significantly enhance your time management skills. Utilize digital calendars, project management software, and task-tracking applications to keep track of your commitments and deadlines. Experiment with different time management techniques such as the Pomodoro Technique, time blocking, or the Eisenhower Matrix to find what works best for you.

Moreover, it is essential to learn how to delegate and outsource tasks that can be done by others. As a creative entrepreneur, your core focus should be on your artistic endeavors and building your career. By delegating non-essential tasks like administrative work or social media management to others, you can free up valuable time to concentrate on what you do best.

Finally, remember to schedule time for self-care and relaxation. The creative industry can be demanding and stressful, and taking care of your well-being is crucial for long-term success. Prioritize activities like exercise, meditation, and spending time with loved ones to recharge and maintain your creativity and productivity.

In conclusion, managing time and priorities is a vital skill for every creative entrepreneur. By setting clear goals, prioritizing tasks, utilizing productivity tools, and delegating when necessary, you can make the most of your time and thrive in your creative career. Remember, time is your most precious resource, so use it wisely and purposefully to achieve your artistic aspirations.

Setting SMART Goals for Artistic Success

In the creative industry, setting goals is crucial for aspiring artists to achieve long-term success in their careers. However, it's not just about setting any goals; it's about setting SMART goals. SMART stands for Specific, Measurable, Achievable, Relevant, and Time-bound – a framework to help artists focus their efforts and maximize their potential. In this subchapter, we will delve into the importance of setting SMART goals and how it can propel students towards a successful artistic career.

Specific goals are essential for artists because they provide clarity and direction. Instead of setting a vague goal like "become a successful artist," students should define specific objectives such as "create an art portfolio showcasing my unique style and submit it to at least five galleries by the end of the year." By being specific, artists can better plan their actions and measure their progress effectively.

Measurable goals help artists track their advancement and stay motivated. Metrics like the number of artworks created, the number of exhibitions attended, or the amount of income generated can provide tangible evidence of an artist's growth. Having measurable goals also allows students to identify areas where they need improvement, fostering a continuous learning mindset.

Achievable goals are realistic and attainable. While it's crucial to dream big, setting goals that are too far-fetched can lead to disappointment and frustration. Instead, students should set objectives that challenge them but are within their reach. For example, aspiring musicians can set a goal of performing at local venues before aiming for larger music festivals.

Relevant goals align with an artist's long-term aspirations and values. It's crucial for students to reflect on their artistic vision and purpose. By setting goals that resonate with their core values, artists can ensure that their efforts are not in vain. For instance, a painter who values environmental sustainability may set a goal of using only eco-friendly materials in their artwork.

Time-bound goals have a deadline or timeframe attached to them. Without a sense of urgency, goals can easily be put off or abandoned. By setting specific dates or timeframes, artists can hold themselves accountable and work towards their goals consistently. It also helps in breaking down larger goals into smaller, manageable tasks.

In conclusion, setting SMART goals is vital for students pursuing a career in the creative industry. By being specific, measurable, achievable, relevant, and time-bound, artists can focus their efforts, track their progress, and stay motivated. Setting SMART goals serves as a road map towards artistic success and enables students to thrive in their chosen fields.

Maintaining Work-Life Balance in a Demanding Industry

In the fast-paced and demanding world of the creative industry, achieving a healthy work-life balance can often be a challenge. As students preparing to embark on a career in this field, it is crucial to understand the importance of maintaining this balance to ensure long-term success and personal fulfillment.

One of the key reasons why work-life balance is so crucial in a demanding industry is the potential for burnout. The creative industry is known for its tight deadlines, intense competition, and high expectations, which can easily lead to stress and exhaustion. Without a proper balance between work and personal life, it becomes increasingly difficult to sustain productivity and creativity over time. Therefore, finding ways to recharge and disconnect from work is essential for maintaining mental and physical well-being.

To achieve work-life balance, it is important to set boundaries and establish priorities. As a student preparing for a career in the creative industry, it can be tempting to throw yourself fully into your work and neglect other aspects of your life. However, it is crucial to remember that maintaining a well-rounded life outside of work actually enhances your creativity and productivity in the long run. By setting clear boundaries between work and personal life, such as designating specific work hours and creating a dedicated workspace, you can create a healthier balance.

Additionally, it is essential to prioritize self-care and make time for hobbies and activities that bring you joy. Engaging in activities outside of work, such as exercising, spending time with loved ones, or pursuing creative passions unrelated to your career, can help reduce stress and foster a sense of fulfillment. Making time for self-care not only improves your overall well-being but also enhances your ability to perform at your best when you are working.

Lastly, seeking support and building a network of like-minded individuals is crucial for maintaining work-life balance in a demanding industry. Surrounding yourself with people who understand the challenges of the creative field and can provide guidance and support can make a significant difference. These connections can offer valuable insights, help you navigate the industry, and remind you that you are not alone in your pursuit of work-life balance.

In conclusion, maintaining work-life balance is vital for students embarking on a career in the demanding creative industry. By setting boundaries, establishing priorities, prioritizing self-care, and seeking support, you can thrive both personally and professionally. Remember, achieving work-life balance is not only essential for your well-being but also enhances your ability to excel in your chosen career path.

Chapter 9: Thriving in the Digital Age

Embracing Technology and Digital Tools for Artists

In today's rapidly evolving digital landscape, technology has become an integral part of our lives, and the world of art is no exception. As aspiring artists and students looking to build a successful career in the creative industry, it is vital to understand and harness the power of technology and digital tools to enhance your artistic abilities and stay competitive in the ever-changing market.

One of the most significant advantages of embracing technology as an artist is the ability to reach a broader audience. With the rise of social media platforms and online galleries, artists now have the opportunity to showcase their work to a global audience at the click of a button. By creating an online portfolio and engaging with potential clients and art enthusiasts through platforms like Instagram, Facebook, and Twitter, you can gain exposure and build a network that may lead to exciting opportunities and collaborations.

Moreover, technology has revolutionized the way artists create and produce their work. Digital tools such as graphic design software, 3D modeling programs, and virtual reality applications have expanded the possibilities for artistic expression. These tools not only allow for greater experimentation and creativity but also offer more efficient and cost-effective methods of production. As a student eager to establish a successful career, it is crucial to familiarize yourself with these digital tools and continually update your skills to stay relevant in the industry.

Furthermore, technology has also opened up new avenues for artists to monetize their work. With the rise of e-commerce platforms and print-on-demand services, artists can now sell their creations directly to consumers worldwide, without the need for intermediaries. Additionally, crowdfunding platforms have emerged as a popular way for artists to fund their projects and connect with patrons who believe in their vision.

However, it is important to strike a balance between embracing technology and maintaining your artistic integrity. While technology offers endless possibilities, it's essential to remember that it is merely a tool. The core of your artistic practice should always be driven by your unique voice, creativity, and passion.

In conclusion, embracing technology and digital tools as an artist is not just an option but a necessity in today's digital age. By leveraging the power of technology to reach a wider audience, enhance your artistic capabilities, and explore new avenues for monetization, you can position yourself for success in the creative industry. As a student, staying up to date with the latest technological advancements and continuously honing your skills will give you a competitive edge and help you thrive in your artistic journey.

Establishing an Online Presence and E-commerce Platform

In today's digital age, having a strong online presence is essential for any artistic entrepreneur looking to thrive in the creative industry. Whether you are a photographer, designer, writer, or musician, the internet provides an unprecedented opportunity to showcase your work, connect with potential clients or customers, and even sell your products or services directly through e-commerce platforms. This subchapter will guide students on how to establish a solid online presence and create an effective e-commerce platform to boost their careers in the creative industry.

The first step in establishing an online presence is to create a professional website or portfolio. This will serve as your digital storefront, where potential clients or customers can explore your work and learn more about your artistic journey. Invest time in creating a visually appealing and user-friendly website that reflects your unique style and showcases your best works. Include a well-written biography or artist statement to give visitors a glimpse into your background and artistic vision.

Additionally, it is crucial to leverage social media platforms to expand your online presence. Identify the platforms that resonate most with your target audience and regularly post engaging and high-quality content. Use these platforms to share behind-the-scenes glimpses of your creative process, promote your upcoming projects or events, and interact with your followers. Building a strong and engaged social media following can significantly boost your visibility and attract potential clients or customers.

When it comes to selling your products or services online, e-commerce platforms are a game-changer. Choose a reliable platform that aligns with your needs and budget, such as Shopify, Etsy, or Squarespace. These platforms provide easy-to-use templates and tools to set up your online store, manage inventory, process payments, and even handle shipping and customer support. Ensure that your product descriptions and images are captivating and accurately represent your work.

Lastly, don't forget to optimize your online presence for search engines. Implement basic search engine optimization (SEO) techniques, such as using relevant keywords in your website's content and meta tags. This will help potential clients or customers find you more easily when they search for specific keywords related to your artistic niche.

By establishing a strong online presence and creating an effective e-commerce platform, students can significantly enhance their careers in the creative industry. Embrace the digital realm, showcase your unique talents, and connect with a global audience that appreciates and supports your artistic endeavors.

Engaging with Online Communities and Art Platforms

In today's digital age, the creative industry has witnessed a significant shift towards online communities and art platforms. As aspiring artists and creative entrepreneurs, it is crucial for students to understand the importance of engaging with these platforms to thrive in their careers.

Online communities and art platforms offer a plethora of opportunities for artists to showcase their work, connect with fellow creators, and gain exposure to a wider audience. These platforms act as virtual galleries, allowing artists to display their art, share their creative process, and receive feedback from a global community of art enthusiasts.

One of the key benefits of engaging with online communities and art platforms is the ability to network with like-minded individuals. By joining these platforms, students can connect with fellow artists, art collectors, and industry professionals who can provide valuable insights, collaborations, and potential career opportunities. Sharing ideas, receiving constructive criticism, and collaborating with others can greatly enhance one's artistic skills and broaden their creative horizons.

Furthermore, these platforms serve as powerful marketing tools for aspiring artists. By showcasing their work online, students can establish their personal brand and attract potential clients, galleries, and employers. Platforms like Instagram, Behance, and DeviantArt offer artists the chance to curate their own online portfolio, allowing them to present their work in a professional and visually appealing manner.

Engaging with online communities and art platforms also provides students with the opportunity to stay updated with the latest trends and industry news. By actively participating in discussions, following influential artists, and staying connected to the creative community, students can gain valuable insights into emerging artistic styles, techniques, and market demands. This knowledge can help them adapt, innovate, and stay ahead in their careers.

It is important for students to approach these platforms with a strategic mindset. Regularly updating their profiles, actively participating in discussions, and consistently sharing their work can significantly increase their visibility and engagement. Additionally, students should be mindful of building a positive online presence by engaging in respectful and constructive conversations.

In conclusion, engaging with online communities and art platforms is essential for students looking to build successful careers in the creative industry. By harnessing the power of these platforms, students can showcase their work, connect with industry professionals, gain exposure, and stay updated with the latest trends. Through active participation and strategic use, students can leverage these online communities and art platforms to thrive as artistic entrepreneurs.

Chapter 10: Sustaining Long-Term Success in the Creative Industry

Adapting to Industry Trends and Changes

In the fast-paced and ever-evolving creative industry, it is crucial for students pursuing a career in this field to understand the importance of adapting to industry trends and changes. The ability to recognize and respond to the shifting landscape of the creative industry is a key skill that will not only help students thrive but also ensure their long-term success as artistic entrepreneurs.

The creative industry is known for its dynamic nature, with trends and technologies constantly emerging and transforming the way artists, designers, and creators work. As a student, it is essential to stay informed about the latest trends, innovations, and changes happening within the industry. This will enable you to anticipate shifts in consumer preferences, technological advancements, and market demands, allowing you to stay one step ahead of the competition.

One of the best ways to adapt to industry trends and changes is through continuous learning and professional development. Take advantage of workshops, seminars, and online courses that focus on industry-specific skills and knowledge. By investing in your education, you can refine your craft, expand your skill set, and stay up-to-date with the latest tools and techniques used in your chosen field.

Networking is another crucial aspect of adapting to industry trends and changes. Engage with professionals in your field, attend industry-related events, and join online communities or forums where you can connect with like-minded individuals. Building a strong network not only provides opportunities for collaboration and mentorship but also keeps you informed about the latest happenings, trends, and changes within the industry.

Flexibility and adaptability are also key traits for success in the creative industry. Embrace change and be open to new ideas and ways of doing things. Remember that the creative industry thrives on innovation, and being receptive to change will help you stay relevant and competitive.

Lastly, always keep an eye on the market and consumer behavior. Understanding your target audience and their preferences is crucial for adapting to industry trends and changes. Stay connected with your audience through social media, surveys, and feedback, and use this information to tailor your offerings and strategies accordingly.

In conclusion, adapting to industry trends and changes is paramount for students pursuing a career in the creative industry. By staying informed, continuously learning, networking, and embracing flexibility, students can position themselves as thriving artistic entrepreneurs. Remember, the creative industry is ever-evolving, and those who can adapt and innovate will find long-term success in this dynamic field.

Continuing Education and Skill Enhancement

In the fast-paced and ever-evolving world of the creative industry, the importance of continuing education and skill enhancement cannot be overstated. As a student pursuing a career in the creative field, it is crucial to understand that learning does not stop once you step out of the classroom or graduate from a program. Instead, it is a lifelong journey that requires constant dedication and a thirst for knowledge.

Continuing education goes beyond obtaining a degree or a certificate. It involves actively seeking out opportunities to expand your skillset, deepen your understanding of your chosen field, and stay up-to-date with the latest industry trends and technologies. This commitment to ongoing learning is what sets successful artistic entrepreneurs apart from the rest.

One of the best ways to continue your education is through professional development workshops, seminars, and conferences. These events provide an excellent platform for networking with industry professionals, learning from experts who have already made their mark, and gaining valuable insights into various aspects of the creative industry. Remember, the more you invest in yourself and your education, the more doors will open for you in your career.

Additionally, staying plugged into online communities, forums, and social media groups can provide a wealth of resources for skill enhancement. Engaging with like-minded individuals, participating in discussions, and sharing your own experiences can greatly contribute to your growth as a creative professional. Online platforms also offer a plethora of tutorials, webinars, and courses that can be accessed from anywhere, allowing you to learn at your own pace and convenience.

Furthermore, seeking mentorship from industry veterans can be a game-changer in your career. A mentor can provide guidance, share their experiences, and offer valuable advice that can propel you forward. They can also help you identify areas where you can improve and suggest specific resources or training programs to enhance your skills.

In conclusion, continuing education and skill enhancement are essential for students pursuing a career in the creative industry. By actively seeking out learning opportunities, attending workshops and conferences, engaging in online communities, and seeking mentorship, you are investing in your own success. Remember, the creative industry is constantly evolving, and by staying ahead of the curve, you are positioning yourself for a thriving and fulfilling career as an artistic entrepreneur.

Finding Inspiration and Avoiding Burnout

In the fast-paced and demanding world of the creative industry, it is not uncommon for students pursuing a career in the arts to experience burnout. The constant pressure to produce innovative and original work, coupled with the need to meet deadlines and exceed expectations, can take a toll on even the most passionate individuals. However, by actively seeking out inspiration and adopting healthy habits, students can safeguard their mental and emotional well-being while maintaining their creative edge.

One of the primary keys to avoiding burnout is finding inspiration. Inspiration can come from various sources, such as nature, music, literature, or even everyday experiences. Students should make a conscious effort to explore different avenues that stimulate their creativity. Engaging in activities outside of their field of study can expose them to new ideas and perspectives that can spark inspiration. Attending gallery openings, concerts, or literary events can provide a fresh perspective and invigorate their creative energy.

Another essential aspect of finding inspiration is cultivating a supportive network. Surrounding oneself with like-minded individuals who share a passion for the arts can foster a sense of community and provide a platform for exchanging ideas. Collaborating with peers, attending workshops, or joining art clubs can all contribute to a vibrant creative environment that fuels inspiration.

However, inspiration alone is not enough to sustain a successful career in the creative industry. It is equally crucial to adopt healthy habits that prevent burnout. Students should develop a routine that includes regular breaks, exercise, and sufficient sleep. Taking breaks throughout the day allows for mental rest and prevents exhaustion. Engaging in physical activity not only boosts energy levels but also enhances mood and creativity. Additionally, prioritizing sleep is vital for cognitive function and overall well-being.

Furthermore, learning to manage stress and setting realistic goals are essential in avoiding burnout. Students should identify their limits and recognize when to step back and recharge. It is essential to establish a balance between work and leisure, ensuring time for self-care and relaxation. Setting achievable goals and celebrating small victories along the way can provide a sense of accomplishment and motivation.

In conclusion, finding inspiration and avoiding burnout are two crucial elements for students pursuing a career in the creative industry. By actively seeking inspiration, cultivating a supportive network, and adopting healthy habits, students can safeguard their mental and emotional well-being while thriving in their chosen field. Remember, creativity flourishes when the mind is nourished and nurtured, so make self-care a priority and never underestimate the power of inspiration in fueling your artistic journey.

Conclusion: Your Journey as an Artistic Entrepreneur

Conclusion: Your Journey as an Artistic Entrepreneur

Congratulations! You have reached the end of this insightful journey as an artistic entrepreneur. Throughout this book, we have explored the exciting world of the creative industry, delving into the intricacies of entrepreneurship and how it can be applied to your artistic endeavors. As students preparing to embark on a career in the creative industry, you now possess the knowledge and tools to thrive in this dynamic field.

Becoming an artistic entrepreneur is not an easy path, but it is a rewarding one. It requires a combination of creativity, business acumen, and a strong entrepreneurial mindset. By embracing these qualities, you have the potential to transform your passion for art into a successful and fulfilling career.

One of the key takeaways from this book is the importance of developing your personal brand. As an artist, you are not just selling your work, but also yourself. Your unique perspective, style, and story are what set you apart from the competition. By investing time and effort into defining and refining your personal brand, you can attract the right audience, clients, and opportunities that align with your artistic vision.

Another crucial aspect of your journey as an artistic entrepreneur is building a strong network. Surrounding yourself with like-minded individuals, mentors, and industry professionals can be invaluable in your career growth. Attend industry events, join online communities, and seek out collaborations to expand your network and learn from others who have walked the same path.

As you navigate the creative industry, it is essential to stay adaptable and open to new opportunities. The industry is ever-evolving, and embracing change can lead to exciting ventures and unexpected breakthroughs. Embrace technology, keep up with industry trends, and continuously learn and refine your skills to stay ahead of the curve.

Remember that setbacks and failures are a part of any entrepreneurial journey. Don't be discouraged by challenges; instead, view them as opportunities for growth and learning. Perseverance, resilience, and a positive mindset will be your greatest assets in overcoming obstacles and achieving success.

Finally, never forget the passion and love that brought you to this career path in the first place. The creative industry can be demanding and competitive, but it is also incredibly rewarding. Stay true to your artistic voice, nurture your creativity, and always strive to create work that is meaningful and authentic to you.

As you embark on your journey as an artistic entrepreneur, remember that success is not solely measured by financial gain but also by the impact you make through your art. Embrace the challenges, take risks, and never stop creating. The creative industry is waiting for your unique contribution, so go out there and make your mark!

Good luck on your artistic entrepreneurial journey, and may your creativity flourish in the ever-evolving landscape of the creative industry.

9 788119 747542